Hone

MW00989001

by Martha E. H. Rustad

Consulting Editor: Gail Saunders-Smith, Ph.D.
Consultant: Gary A. Dunn, Director of Education,
Young Entomologists' Society

Pebble Books

an imprint of Capstone Press
Mankato, Minnesota

Pebble Books are published by Capstone Press
1710 Roe Crest Drive, North Mankato, Minnesota 56003
www.capstonepub.com

Library of Congress Cataloging-in-Publication Data
Rustad, Martha E. H. (Martha Elizabeth Hillman), 1975–
    Honey Bees / by Martha E. H. Rustad.
    p. cm. —(Insects)
    Summary: Simple text and photographs present the features and behavior
of honey bees.
    Includes bibliographical references and index.
    13-digit: 978-0-7368-1666-3 (library binding)
    10-digit: 0-7368-1666-6 (library binding)
    13-digit: 978-0-7368-4882-4 (softcover pbk.)
    10-digit: 0-7368-4882-7 (softcover pbk.)
    1. Honeybee—Juvenile literature. [1. Honeybee. 2. Bees.] I. Title. II. Insects
(Mankato, Minn.)
QL568.A6 R87 2003
595.79'9—dc21   2002014149

Note to Parents and Teachers

The Insects series supports national science standards for units on the
diversity and unity of life. The series shows that animals have features that
help them live in different environments. This book describes and
illustrates honey bees and their parts and habits. The photographs support
early readers in understanding the text. The repetition of words and
phrases helps early readers learn new words. This book also introduces
early readers to subject-specific vocabulary words, which are defined in the
Words to Know section. Early readers may need assistance to read some
words and to use the Table of Contents, Words to Know, Read More,
Internet Sites, and Index/Word List sections of the book.

Printed in the United States of America in Stevens Point, Wisconsin.
032015   008807R

Table of Contents

Honey bees have stripes.

Honey bees have
two antennas.

8

Honey bees have
four wings.

small eyes

large eyes

10

Honey bees have
five eyes.

Honey bees live
in hives.

a honey bee hive covered with bees

Honey bees collect pollen and nectar from flowers.

pollen baskets

Honey bees carry
pollen on their legs
in pollen baskets.

proboscis

Honey bees drink nectar
from flowers with
their proboscis.

Honey bees use nectar
to make honey
in their hives.

Words to Know

antenna—a feeler on an insect's head; most insects use their antennas to touch, taste, or smell.

eye—a body part used for seeing; honey bees have two large eyes that are called compound eyes, and three small eyes that are called simple eyes.

hive—a structure where honey bees live; thousands of honey bees may live in a hive.

honey—a sweet, sticky matter that honey bees make from nectar

nectar—a sweet liquid that honey bees gather from flowers

pollen—tiny, yellow grains in flowers

pollen basket—a set of stiff hairs on the back legs of a honey bee where pollen is stored

proboscis—a part of the mouth that honey bees use to gather nectar; a honey bee's proboscis is long and shaped like a tube.

Read More

Heiligman, Deborah. *Honeybees.* Jump into Science. Washington, D.C.: National Geographic Society, 2002.

Holmes, Kevin J. *Bees.* Animals. Mankato, Minn.: Bridgestone Books, 1998.

Schaefer, Lola M. *Honey Bees and Hives.* Honey Bees. Mankato, Minn.: Pebble Books, 1999.

Internet Sites

Track down many sites about honey bees.
Visit the FACT HOUND at *http://www.facthound.com*

IT IS EASY! IT IS FUN!

1) Go to *http://www.facthound.com*

2) Type in: 0736816666

3) Click on "FETCH IT" and FACT HOUND will find several links hand-picked by our editors.

Relax and let our pal FACT HOUND do the research for you!

Index/Word List

Word Count: 61
Early-Intervention Level: 7

Editorial Credits

Hollie J. Endres, editor; Timothy Halldin, cover designer and illustrator;
   Gene Bentdahl and Molly Nei, book designers; Karrey Tweten,
   photo researcher

Photo Credits

Bruce Coleman Inc./Larry West, 1
Digital Vision, 4, 20
Image Ideas, Inc., 14; Paul Hartley, cover
Michael Durham, 6
Stephen McDaniel, 10, 12, 16, 18
Visuals Unlimited/Al, Linda Bristor, 8